A RAISIN IN THE SUN

Lorraine Hansberry

AUTHORED by Cheryl Sherrod
UPDATED AND REVISED by Jordan Berkow

COVER DESIGN by Table XI Partners LLC
COVER PHOTO by Olivia Verma and © 2005 GradeSaver, LLC

BOOK DESIGN by Table XI Partners LLC

Published by GradeSaver LLC, www.gradesaver.com

First published in the United States of America by GradeSaver LLC. 2006

ISBN 978-1-60259-047-2

Printed in the United States of America

For other products and additional information please visit http://www.gradesaver.com

Table of Contents

Table of Contents

Biography of Lorraine Hansberry (1930–1965)

"Black" was the word handwritten on Lorraine Vivian Hansberry's birth certificate on May 19, 1930. The hospital had printed "Negro", but Carl and Nannie Perry Hansberry crossed out the hospital's label and asserted the right to designate their child's racial identity on their own terms. Challenging the system was part of the Hansberrys' way of life. Carl had achieved success in real estate and banking even in the midst of the Great Depression. He and his wife raised four children on the South Side of Chicago. Lorraine was the youngest of these children. Separated from her siblings by seven years, she often played alone. In addition, her family's affluence separated her from her peers. Her father was a successful businessman, and had run for Congress. Her uncle was a well–noted college professor at Howard University. Lastly, her mother, a former school teacher, was a committeewoman. Lorraine often felt the desire to be more like the friends she went to school with. She recalls wearing a roller skate key around her neck so that she could pretend she was a "latchkey" kid.

The Hansberry household was in no way typical to the South Side of Chicago. People like W.E.B. Dubois and Paul Robeson were close family friends, and made frequent visits to the house. In addition to his other accomplishments, Carl Hansberry was very active in the National Association for the Advancement of Colored People (NAACP). When Lorraine was eight years old, the family had just moved into a predominantly white neighborhood, and her father was in the midst of the landmark Supreme Court case *Hansberry v Lee* involving housing discrimination. The Hansberrys won the case, yet still faced many trials. The hostility from the white neighbors grew, and eventually a mob threw bricks and broken concrete into the Hansberrys' house. One of the pieces barely missed young Lorraine's head.

Lorraine graduated from Englewood High School in 1948 and attended the University of Wisconsin. She excelled in the humanities, but struggled with the required science courses. Two years later, Hansberry left college and moved to New York to pursue her writing career. Living on the Lower East Side, Lorraine was free to explore the life of Harlem and Greenwich Village and participated in protests about racial discrimination and various other forms of social injustice. Her first job was as a secretary for *Freedom*, an African–American newspaper founded by activist Paul Robeson. She initially was hired as the secretary, but eventually began writing and editing articles. In particular, she criticized the media's representation of blacks as unintelligent and sub–human. During her time in New York, Hansberry also attended classes at the New School for Social Research, which enabled her to focus more on the subjects of her interest.

In June of 1952, she met a young man named Robert Nemiroff while they were both protesting segregated sports teams at New York University. Nemiroff was the son of

Russian–Jewish immigrants who owned a downtown restaurant, and Hansberry spent many afternoons there with his family and friends. Not long after, on June 20, 1953, Hansberry and Nemiroff were married in Chicago at a ceremony that both families attended. Hansberry worked to support her husband through his graduate studies in literature at New York University by doing several odd jobs, including a two–week camp for adults to promote racial unity. In 1956 Nemiroff was able to achieve financial security when he wrote the hit song "Cindy, O Cindy", and began to help support his wife's writing career.

Hansberry's dedication to writing paid off when her first play won popular and critical acclaim. *A Raisin in the Sun* won the Drama Critics Circle Award for 1958–1959. Hansberry went on to write *Les Blancs* and *The Sign in Sidney Brustein's Window*. Some of her other works include the screenplay *Drinking Gourd* and the autobiographical piece *To Be Young, Gifted, and Black.*

On January 12, 1965, Lorraine Hansberry died an early death at the age of 34 after a struggle with pancreatic cancer. That same night, the curtain closed as *The Sign in Sidney Brustein's Window* gave its last performance. Inscribed on her tombstone is the following passage from the play:

> I care. I care about it all. It takes too much energy not to care...The *why* of why we are here is an intrigue for adolescents; the *how* is what must command the living. Which is why I have lately become an insurgent again.

About A Raisin in the Sun

Lorraine Hansberry, in an August 1959 *Village Voice* article, wrote:

> In an almost paradoxical fashion, it disturbs the soul of man to truly understand what he invariably senses: that nobody really finds oppression and/or poverty tolerable. If we ever destroy the image of the black people who supposedly do find those things tolerable in America, then that much–touted "guilt" which allegedly haunts most middle–class white Americans with regard to the Negro question would really become unendurable.

Combating the myth of complacency is the central idea that drives Hansberry's play. During a time when African–Americans were portrayed in musicals as jovial resilient characters who were content with their status, *A Raisin in the Sun* emerged as the first drama written and produced by an African–American that challenged this myth of contentment. On March 11, 1959, Lorraine Vivian Hansberry had her captive audience. That night was not just another evening at the theatre, but rather marked the beginning of a conversation about several vital issues that concerned not just blacks, but the American people as a whole. In this play, Hansberry vividly portrays the stress of poverty. On stage, she creates a real world where five humans are squeezed into a one–bedroom apartment, where a young boy must scramble for a measly fifty cents, and where a man must die for the family to have any hope for the future.

On the surface, Broadway seemed ready to embrace a play like *A Raisin in the Sun.* At the age of 29, Lorraine Hansberry was the first and youngest African–American to receive the New York Drama Critics Circle Award (for 1958–1959). However, *A Raisin in the Sun* won the Drama Circle's Critics Award by only one vote. Although it is now considered an American classic, *Raisin* did not achieve such critical acclaim without controversy. At the same time, Tennessee William's *Sweet Bird of Youth*, Eugene O' Neill's *A Touch of the Poet* and Archibald MacLeish's *J.B.* were playing on Broadway. Hansberry's straightforward social realism stood out amidst the psychological dramas of the time. Interestingly, the play was also not well received by African–Americans with more militant political views. Critic Harold Cruse said of the play,

> *A Raisin in the Sun* expressed through the medium of theatrical art that current, forced symbiosis in American interracial affairs wherein the Negro working class has been roped in and tied to the chariot of racial integration driven by the Negro middle class. In this drive for integration the Negro working class is being told in a thousand ways that it must give up its ethnicity and become human, universal full–fledged American.

Cruse, an anti–integrationist, feared that integration's goal of acceptance into the majority culture would come at the cost of African–Americans' ethnicity. Another critic, fellow playwright Amiri Baraka, who initially dismissed the play's significance, recanted years later and recognized its importance. Baraka said in 1987, "The Younger family is part of the black majority, and the concerns I once dismissed as "middle class"– buying a house and moving into "white folks' neighborhoods"–are actually reflective of the essence of black people's striving to defeat segregation, discrimination, and national oppression." Ironically, the words of this former critic best capture the Youngers' contribution to American theatre.

When *A Raisin in the Sun* opened in 1959 at the Ethel Barrymore Theatre, three major adaptations from the original script had been made. In order to cut costs, the scene with Mrs. Johnson, the Youngers' nosy and pretentious neighbor, was cut. The scene previously served to reinforce the various forms of opposition that the Youngers might face. Technical problems also caused the crucial "natural hair" scene to be cut from the production. Originally Beneatha is supposed to cut her hair into a natural style that Asagai admires. However, just before the opening, actress Diana Sands, who played Beneatha, got a haircut that was so bad that the cast felt it would negate the positive attitude toward natural hair that Hansberry was trying to convey. The last omission from the original work was the scene where Travis and his friends chase a rat through the neighborhood. In 1960, a film version of *A Raisin in the Sun* was released with many more deviations from the original. Walter does not just talk about the local bar, the Green Hat; he is actually *shown* in it. Also, the Younger family is actually shown moving into the new house. In 1973, Robert Nemiroff revised the play as a musical that ran on Broadway for two years, winning both a Tony and a Grammy.

Character List

A 35–year–old chauffeur who has a young son, Travis, with his wife, Ruth. The family lives in small apartment with Walter's mother and sister in the South Side of Chicago. Hansberry describes Walter as a lean, intense man with nervous movements and erratic speaking patterns. Played by Sidney Poitier in the original Broadway production.

The 60–something matriarch of the family. She has recently lost her husband Walter Sr., and will be the recipient of a $10,000 life insurance check. Played by Claudia McNeil in the original Broadway production.

Walter's 20–year–old sister, a college student who invades the Younger household with her modern ideas and philosophies on race, class, and religion. She is a handsome intellectual who has worked hard to refine her speech. Played by Diana Sands in the original Broadway production.

Walter's wife and Travis' mother. In her early thirties, Ruth is exceptionally pretty, but is aging before her time because of her impoverished surroundings. During her 11 years of marriage, she often bore the responsibility of keeping the household running, in addition to working as a domestic servant. Played by Ruby Dee in the original Broadway production.

Walter and Ruth's 10–year–old son.

A Nigerian college student pursuing Beneatha.

Beneatha's boyfriend and fellow classmate, who hails from a wealthy black family.

The Youngers' nosy neighbor, who points out the dangers of moving into Clybourne Park

A white, middle–aged representative from the Clybourne Park Improvement Society.

A fellow investor in the liquor business, along with Willy and Walter.

A partner in the liquor business scheme who eventually runs off with Walter and Bob's investment money.

Major Themes

The long–standing appeal of *A Raisin in the Sun* lies in the fact that the family's dreams and aspirations for a better life are not confined to their race, but can be identified with by people of all backgrounds. Even though what that "better life" may look like is different for each character, the underlying motivation is universal. The central conflict of the play lies in Walter's notion of this American dream. Walter buys into the middle–class ideology of materialism. The notion of the self–made man who starts with nothing and achieves great wealth through hard work seems innocuous enough, but the idea can become pernicious if it evolves into an idolization of wealth and power. In the beginning, Hansberry shows how Walter envies Charlie Atkins' dry–cleaning business because it grosses $100,000 a year. He ignores Ruth's objection to his potential business partner's questionable character and dismisses his mother's moral objection to achieving his goals by running a liquor store. The liquor store is a means to an end, and Walter is desperate for his dreams to come to fruition. That same Machiavellian ethic is demonstrated when Walter plans to accept Mr. Lindner's offer. Walter is not concerned with the degrading implications of the business deal. It is simply a way to recover some of the lost money. However, Hansberry challenges Walter's crude interpretation of the American dream by forcing him to actually carry out the transaction in front of his son. Walter's inability to deal with Mr. Lindner marks a significant revision of his interpretation of the American dream, a dream that inherently prioritizes justice and equality over money.

Three generations of women are represented in *A Raisin in the Sun*. Lena, who is in her early thirties, becomes the default head of the household upon the passing of her husband, Walter Sr. Raised in the South during an era where blacks' very lives were in danger because of the prevalence of lynching, Lena moved to the North with the hopes of leading a better life. The move up North was significant in that she had hopes of a better life for herself. Although Lena is ahead of her times in some respects, her dreams and aspirations are largely linked to her family's well–being, rather than to her own. Scholar Claudia Tate attributes Lena's low expectations for her individual self to gender conditioning – a term used to describe the expectation that a woman's goals and dreams be linked to her family alone. Lena tolerates her husband's womanizing and remains loyal to him even though they suffer under the same impoverished conditions throughout their marriage.

Walter's wife, Ruth, is in her early thirties. She is different from Lena in that she vocalizes her frustrations with her spouse, Walter. Ultimately, however, she seeks to please him, talking positively about the business to Lena on his behalf, encouraging Beneatha not to antagonize her brother so much, and being willing to work several jobs so that the family can afford to move into the new house.

Beneatha, a young feminist college student, is the least tolerant of society's unequal treatment and expectations of women. Beneatha constantly challenges Walter's chauvinism, and has no time for shallow men like George Murchison, who do not respect her ideas. Through these three women, Hansberry skillfully illustrates how women's ideas about their identity have changed over time.

"What defines a man?" is a critical question that Hansberry struggles with throughout the entire play. In many ways, the most debilitating affronts Walter faces are those which relate to his identity as a man, whether it be in his role as father, husband, or son. Being a father to Travis appears to be the role that Walter values the most. He sincerely wants to be perceived as honorable in his son's eyes. Knowing the family has little money to spare, Walter gives Travis a dollar when he asks for fifty cents. Walter chooses the liquor store investment not just to make more money for himself, but also to be better able to provide for his wife and family. He wants to be able to give Ruth pearls and a Cadillac convertible; he wants to be able to send his son to the college of his choice. As a son, he wants to walk in his father's footsteps and provide for his mother in her old age. Walter is framed by the examples of his father and son. At first, Walter is willing to degrade himself in order to obtain these goals, but he faces a critical turning point when he reconsiders Mr. Lindner's offer. Ultimately, he chooses the honorable path so that he can stand before his son Travis with pride.

There is a strong motif of afrocentrism throughout the play. Unlike many of her black contemporaries, Lorraine Hansberry grew up in a family that was well aware of its African heritage, and embraced its roots. Lorraine's uncle, Leo Hansberry, was a professor of African history at Howard University, a well–known, historically black college in Washington, D.C. Hansberry's uncle actually taught Kwame Nkrumah, a revolutionary who fought for the independence of the Gold Coast from British rule. Hansberry's afrocentrism is expressed mainly through Beneatha's love for Asagai. Asagai, a Nigerian native, is who Beneatha seeks out during her search for her own identity. She is eager to learn about African culture, language, music, and dress. The playwright is well ahead of her times in her creation of these characters. Hansberry is able to dispel many of the myths about Africa, and concretely depict the parallel struggles both Africans and African–Americans must face.

A Raisin in the Sun is not just about race; class tensions are a prominent issue throughout the play. George Murchison is Beneatha's well–to–do boyfriend. Although he is educated and wealthy, Beneatha is still trying to sort out her feelings about him. Her sister–in–law, Ruth, does not understand Beneatha's ambivalence: he is good–looking, and able to provide well for Beneatha. However, Beneatha is planning to be a doctor, and is not dependent on "marrying well" for her financial security. Hansberry also hints that marriage into the Murchison family is not very probable. Beneatha says, "Oh, Mama– The Murchisons are honest–to–God–real–*live*–rich colored people, and the only people in the world who are more snobbish than rich white people are rich colored people. I thought everybody knew that I've met Mrs. Murchison. She's a scene!" Beneatha is sensitive to the reality that even though the two families are black, they are deeply divided. Beneatha suggests that class distinctions are more pronounced amongst African–Americans than between African–Americans and whites. Despite their degree of wealth or education, blacks in America were discriminated against. Wealthy African–Americans had limitations on schools, housing, and occupations just like their poor counterparts. Mrs. Murchison's 'snobbishness' is emblematic of a desperate yet futile attempt to be seen as different from poor blacks and thus gain acceptance by whites. However, radical legislative and social change proves to be the only substantive solution to America's problem.

Glossary of Terms

The largest tribe in Ghana, the Ashanti grew to prominence due to the wealth of iron and gold found in their country before the rival Mali tribe put an end to the Ghana Empire in 1180.

One of the longest–lasting civilizations in West Africa, the kingdom's art centered on sculpture that recounted historical events. Utilizing bronze, ivory, or terra cotta, this style was influential because of its high degree of realism and stylization.

Known for his innovative and revolutionary battle formations, this great military warrior built the Zulu tribe into a powerful nation that united against colonial powers in the early nineteenth century.

Earlier called Abyssinia, the country is located in northeastern Africa. Having enjoyed a long history of trade with the Middle East, Ethiopia has been referenced in many sources, from Homer to the Bible. Ethiopia is unique in that it avoided much of the colonial rule experienced by its neighboring African countries, with the exception of a short Italian occupation from 1935–1941.

The term originates from *gheto*, an island off the coast of Italy where Jews were forced to live. Today, it refers to a portion of the city where an ethnic group is forced to live due to socio–economic pressures.

The Mali Empire was the most wealthy and prominent in Africa from about 1100–1500, when it was conquered by the Songhai Empire. Present–day Mali is a landlocked West African nation that was invaded by France in 1880 and, along with Senegal, gained its independence in 1960.

French phrase meaning "Mister small businessman"

A 1942 Oscar–winning film that starred Greer Garson as a English bourgeoisie wife during WWII. Mrs. Miniver appeared tending roses in many of the scenes.

The largest and possibly the most diverse country in Africa, with approximately 130 million people and 250 different ethnic groups. The two major ethnic groups in the south of Nigeria are the Ibo and Yoruba people. In the past Nigeria has been ruled by several colonial powers, including the Portugese, Spainards, and the British. In 1963, Nigeria gained its independence from Britain.

Popularized by "The Lion Sleeps Tonight" by Pete Seeger and the Weavers, the term refers to the title of an African chant about the waking of a lion.

A figure from Greek mythology most noted for stealing fire from the gods and giving it to the humans. Prometheus was punished by being tied to Mount Caucasus, where his liver to be picked out daily by an eagle. *Prometheus Bound* by Aeschylus became highly regarded by Romantic writers like Percy Shelley, and the figure is emblematic for his defiance against the gods.

Farmers who live on someone else's land and pay a disproportionate share of their crop as rent, leaving little for their families to live on.

After Songhai conquered the Mali Empire in 1470, Timbuktu became the center of education and commerce in the Muslim world. At its zenith, the Songhai Empire reached from modern–day Nigeria to parts of the Atlantic coast in the West. However, by the 1600s the empire had disintegrated into several smaller kingdoms.

A poor neighborhood in Chicago where many blacks lived; also known as "the ghetto".

Short Summary

The Youngers are a poor African–American family living on the South Side of Chicago. An opportunity to escape from poverty comes in the form of a $10,000 life insurance check that the matriarch of the family (Lena Younger or Mama) receives upon her husband's death. Lena's children, Walter and Beneatha, each have their plans for the money. The oldest son, Walter (a man of 35 with a wife and a young son), wishes to invest in a liquor store. The younger sister, Beneatha, currently a college student, wants to use the money for medical school. Lena has plans as well for the money: she wants to buy a house for the family and finance Beneatha's medical school.

The environmental pressures are high: five people live in a tiny one–bedroom apartment, two families share a single bathroom, and the building is run–down and roach–infested. These pressures increase when Walter's wife, Ruth, finds out that she is pregnant for the second time, and begins seriously contemplating abortion. Yet even in an environment where a request for fifty cents becomes a family conflict, there is room for ideas and dreams.

Beneatha Younger is the source of the many of the new ideas and philosophies that infiltrate the family's home. Currently in college, she is constantly challenging the notions of culture, race, gender, and religion that her family has grown up with. She is dating two men who represent very different aspects of African–American culture. George Murchison, the first, is a wealthy African–American classmate of Beneatha's. Through his character, Hansberry is able to illustrate many of the class tensions that exist within the African–American culture. Asagai is her second boyfriend, a college student who is from Nigeria. Through Asagai, Beneatha is able to learn more about her African heritage. He gives her Nigerian robes and music, encourages her idealistic aspirations, and near the end of the play invites her to return to Nigeria with him to practice medicine there.

Walter Younger truly encapsulates the American dream. He has a genuine entrepreneurial spirit and desire to progress. Walter doesn't want to challenge the present system as Beneatha does. Instead, he wishes to progress up the social ladder into a higher class. He is unsatisfied with his job as a chauffeur, and wants a big house, a nice car, pearls for his wife, and an office job. In short, he desires the bourgeoisie lifestyle. Walter's idolization of wealth and power actually creates a deep hunger within him for change, but as long as obstacles like racism keep him stagnated, his hopes and dreams fester. After several events, Mama realizes the significance of his plans even though she morally objects to the idea of a liquor store.

After having made the down payment on a house in a predominantly white neighborhood, Lena gives her oldest son responsibility over the rest of the insurance money, asking him to put away a significant portion for his sister's medical school education. To the contrary, Walter decides to invest all the money in the liquor store business with two men of questionable character. The plan falls through when Willy, one of the "investors", runs away with all of the money.

The family is entirely dependent on the money: they already have made plans to move, and are in the midst of packing up their things. Devastated, Walter seriously considers taking an offer from Mr. Lindner, a representative from the white neighborhood, that would pay the Youngers extra not to move into their neighborhood. The option is immoral in the family's eyes, and prioritizes money over human dignity. Walter is determined to make the deal despite his scruples, but at the last moment Walter is unable to make the transaction under the innocent gaze of his son, Travis. In the end, the family decides to move. Even though the road ahead will be difficult, they know that they have made an honorable choice.

Summary and Analysis of Act I scene i

The furniture in the Youngers' apartment is old and worn, but clean. The pattern on the carpet is threadbare; the couch is covered with dollies. Although it is only a one–bedroom apartment, five people live there. Beneatha and Mama live in the bedroom. Walter and his wife Ruth have converted the small breakfast nook into their bedroom. Their son Travis sleeps on the sofa in the living room, which serves as the dining area in the daytime. The multiple functions of the room present a challenge for young Travis. The night before the play begins, Travis has been up late because his father had friends over and the young boy was not able to go to sleep until they left.

Ruth is responsible for getting her son and husband up before cooking breakfast for the family. The Youngers' mornings are rushed. The fact that they share a bathroom with the Johnsons only increases the difficulty of getting to school and work on time. Within the first few moments of the play, the audience is not only exposed to the Youngers' morning routine, but also becomes aware of the extent of the financial pressure on them. Travis needs fifty cents for school, but Ruth refuses because she knows the family cannot spare the money. Travis offers to carry groceries in order to earn the money, but it is beginning to get cold outside, and Ruth is concerned for her son's health. Walter gives his son a dollar anyway, in order to give him the impression that they are not financially strained.

Walter desperately dreams of bettering his situation. Just the night before, Walter was up late talking and planning with friends. He wants to go into business with his friend Willy Harris, whom Ruth calls a "good–for–nothing loud–mouth." He is determined to finally follow through on his plans because he missed out on the last opportunity to start a dry–cleaning business. The owner, Charlie Atkins, now grosses about $100,000 a year. Walter's plan for a liquor store requires an investment of $75,000. The initial investment of $30,000 would be split between three partners, and would consume the whole of the $10,000 life insurance check left to the family by Walter Sr.

While Walter tries to tell Ruth (who is tired and reluctant to listen) about his plans, his sister wakes up and enters the kitchen. Beneatha is a 20–year–old college student, and has a combative relationship with her older brother. She is determined to be a doctor, but Walter is doubtful about the idea. Few women, he declares, decide to become doctors rather than nurses. Ultimately, however, he is concerned about the cost of medical school, and how the burden will infringe upon his dreams. While arguing, he says to Beneatha, "go be a nurse like other women–or just get married and be quiet."

Walter leaves for work and must ask Ruth for fifty cents to take a taxi because he has given Travis all his money. Mama, a robust woman in her early sixties, enters. She is immediately concerned about the well–being of others. She is worried that Beneatha will catch cold without a robe, and about whether Travis got a hot breakfast. After inquiring about the subject of Walter's and Beneatha's argument, Mama notices that Ruth is looking thin and tired. Mama even cares for a little plant that becomes a small but important symbol in the play.

Ruth initiates the conversation about what Mama will do with the insurance check. Just as Walter has asked her to do, Ruth tries to persuade her mother–in–law to invest the money in the liquor store. When Mama asserts that the family is not the investing type, Ruth says, "Ain't nobody business people until they go into business." Despite these words, Ruth encourages Mama to do whatever she wishes with the money, such as travel to Europe. Mama says that she has always wanted a house, and wishes to use the money to make a down payment on a bigger place. Walter Sr. and Mama had always planned to live in a house: the plan was to live in the apartment for a year, and then move to Morgan Park. The dream never came to fruition during Big Walter's lifetime.

Beneatha enters the scene annoyed by the vacuum cleaner being run in the upstairs apartment and exclaims, "Christ's sake!" Mama reprimands Beneatha for swearing. Beneatha reveals to her family that she plans to take up the guitar. Ruth and Mama tease her because Beneatha has taken up so many short–lived hobbies, including horseback riding and photography. Beneatha defends their derision by saying that they are all used to "express" her. Ruth and Mama laugh again and inquire about her courtship with George. Beneatha is dating a wealthy college student named George, but believes he is shallow. George also is not supportive of her desire to become a doctor. Mama emphasizes God's role in her becoming a doctor, and Beneatha dryly responds, "God has nothing to do with it." Mama addresses Beneatha's atheism, warning her that she and her father raised her to believe in God. Beneatha succinctly denounces God as only an idea that she does not believe in. Mama slaps her and makes her repeat, "In my mother's house there is still God." After Beneatha leaves, Mama sadly reflects on the changed relationships between herself and her children, and realizes that she no longer understands them fully.

Analysis

Playwright Amiri Baraka describes Lorraine Hansberry as a "*critical realist* [who] *analyzes* and *assesses* reality and shapes her statement as an aesthetically powerful and politically advanced work of art." The first scene of *A Raisin in the Sun* creates this realistic setting. Following a history of blacks being portrayed on Broadway as happy, jovial, and exotic, Hansberry seeks to debunk this myth of contentment by portraying the realities of poverty and the concrete obstacles racism places in front of the achievement of the American dream.

The set in *A Raisin in the Sun* is critical to this goal, giving the audience a visual testament to the Youngers' poverty. The apartment the Youngers live in has been relentlessly cleaned over the years. The carpet is threadbare from vacuuming; the furniture is worn from dusting; the apartment is sprayed weekly to keep roaches away. Despite their efforts, the facilities are inadequate. The apartment is overcrowded, and one small bathroom serves two large families. During this scene, Hansberry refuses to allow these inadequacies to be forgotten and fade into the background; they constantly disrupt the plot as Travis, Walter, and Beneatha carry on various conversations while keeping an eye out for the bathroom to be free.

The pressures of everyday life in the ghetto have taken a toll on Ruth: "disappointment has already begun to hang in her face." In addition to working as a domestic servant, she is responsible for keeping her family together. Ruth is concerned about the necessities, such as getting the family up on time, making breakfast for her son and husband, and having enough money to get to and from work. She does not have time for world events or Walter's pipe dreams. When Walter begins to talk about his liquor store investment, she responds, "Eat your eggs." When he says how disappointed he is that he can only tell his ten–year–old son stories about rich white people, Ruth again responds, "Eat your eggs." After Walter explodes, Ruth explains:

> Honey, you never say nothing new. I listen to you every day, every night and every morning, and you never say nothing new. (*shrugging*) So you would rather *be* Mr. Arnold than be his chauffeur. So–I would *rather* be living in Buckingham Palace.

Ruth is stifled by the absurd redundancy of everyday life. For the eleven years of her marriage, she has seen no real progression. The Younger family is the epitome of the American work ethic: even though they toil, they do not see the fruits of their labor. In fact, Ruth is not only responding to the disappointments of her lifetime, but to the disappointments experienced by previous generations, as well. Walter Sr. had moved into the same apartment with the hopes of owning a house within a year. Now Walter Sr. has passed, and three generations live in the same tiny apartment. Ruth, overcome by this stagnation, has lost hope.

Both Walter and Beneatha are sustained by their dreams. Walter dreams of being an entrepreneur. He, along with his friends Willy and Bobo, plan to open up a liquor store. Beneatha, currently a college student, wants to become a doctor. Both of these dreams rely upon their father's life insurance check for its realization. Therefore, beneath the seemingly normal brother–sister dissent lies a fierce struggle for the survival of each individual's dreams. This tension surfaces the morning before the insurance check arrives. Walter's deceptively simple inquiry about how Beneatha's studies are going in school leads to an argument. Walter accuses Beneatha of being ungrateful for the sacrifices the family has made for her to go to college. For the first time he reveals that he wishes his sister would "be a nurse…or just get married and be quiet." Walter's chauvinist statement is an open affront to Beneatha, who is struggling to go beyond what society says women ought to do. Walter's dreams for his sister are no bigger than society's. The argument ends with both siblings admitting that the insurance money belongs to Mama, and it is for her to decide how it will be spent. However, the scales are weighed against Walter because his mother is not likely to support the idea of a liquor store.

Both Walter and Beneatha battle with Mama's conservative Protestant ethic. Mama disapproves of Walter's business plan because she disapproves of selling liquor. She says, "Well–whether they drinks it or not ain't none of my business. But whether I go into business selling it to 'em *is*, and I don't want that on my ledger this late in life." Lena's objection is short and succinct: she notifies Beneatha of her moral conviction, and does not seek to debate its validity. Mama's rigid beliefs conflict with Beneatha's new philosophies. When Beneatha asserts that God is just an idea that she does not believe in, Mama slaps Beneatha across the face, giving her daughter the clear message that atheism will not be tolerated in her household.

Summary and Analysis of Act I scene ii

The Younger house is full of anticipation as the family awaits the arrival of the insurance check. Mama cleans the kitchen as Beneatha sprays for cockroaches. Travis, finished with his chores, wants to go outside and play. Beneatha and Travis all inquire where Ruth has gone this morning, and discover that she is at the doctor. The phone rings: Beneatha's friend Asagai wants to come over. Even though the house is messy, Beneatha allows him to come because Asagai does not let superficial things influence his judgment. Mama, however, is not pleased because she feels her house is a reflection of herself. Beneatha then begins to deliver a diatribe about Asagai's native country so that Beneatha will not be embarrassed by her mother's comments. Asagai, Beneatha tells her mother, is from Nigeria. Beneatha informs her mother that even though she donates money to missionary workers in Africa, the real threat to Africa is colonialism.

Ruth comes home from the doctor and despairingly announces that she is pregnant. Mama is enthusiastic about any new member of the family, but both Beneatha and Ruth are worried about finding the resources with which to provide for the child. Ruth has already inquired about getting an abortion. The conversation is interrupted when Travis gets into trouble for chasing rats with his friends.

Asagai arrives carrying a large package. He greets Beneatha as Alaiyo. Asagai has just returned from his studies in Canada, but is more interested in discussing their relationship than his studies. While Asagai knows how he feels, Beneatha still needs time to figure out whether she loves him in return. Asagai gives Beneatha a Nigerian robe and promises to teach her how to drape it. Asagai's light comment about her straightened hair sparks a debate. Asagai feels that Beneatha's decision to straighten her hair rather than wear it naturally, in an afro, is symptomatic of the broader problem of assimilation amongst blacks in the United States. Beneatha adamantly denies being an assimilationist. Asagai dismisses her serious nature in a paternalistic manner and returns to the topic of their relationship.

As Beneatha again reasserts her feminist viewpoints, Mama enters the room and the conversation shifts. Beneatha introduces Lena to Asagai. Mama, determined to prove to her daughter that she understands her modern viewpoints on Africa, recites Beneatha's previous tutorial on the injustice of Africa's colonialism and the infiltration of Christianity. Having "flashed a superior look at her daughter upon completion of her recitation, " Lena becomes truly sympathetic towards Asagai. She looks at him like her own son, asking him if he misses his mom and inviting him to come over to eat since he is so far away from home. Over the course of the conversation, Asagai calls Beneatha "Alaiyo", which in Yoruba means "One for Whom Bread Is Not Enough."

Asagai leaves, and the family returns their attention to the insurance check. The check arrives, and Travis brings it to his grandmother. The family is at first very excited, checking to make sure the amount is correct. Then, the gravity of the situation hits Lena. As she realizes this the compensation for her husband's life, she sobers and says, "Ten thousand dollars they give you. Ten thousand dollars."

After Travis leaves, Lena inquires more about Ruth's doctor visit. Lena senses something is amiss, but Walter soon enters and is too preoccupied by the insurance check to be worried about his wife. Walter excitedly brings up the liquor store investment, but Mama shoots him down immediately. Walter, upset, gets up to leave. Ruth, wanting to talk to him, gets her coat too. Frustrated and unable to reason with him, Ruth goes into the bedroom.

Lena, disturbed by the relationship between her son and her daughter–in–law, tries to figure out what is going on with Walter. Walter expresses how he is tired of his situation and wants to make more money. He says, BLOCKQUOTE [Mama–sometimes when I'm downtown and I pass them cool, quiet–looking restaurants where them white boys are sitting back and talking 'bout things…sitting there turning deals worth millions of dollars...] Mama is frustrated with Walter's obsession with money. She tries to put things in perspective, and talks about when freedom used to be the most important thing to their ancestors. Walter still objects, and as a last attempt to put things in perspective, Lena tells her son that Ruth is pregnant and has been considering getting an abortion. Ruth, having just come out of the bedroom, confirms the story. Lena expects her son to be enraged and to talk some sense into Ruth, but Walter is speechless. Lena, in turn, becomes furious. As Walter walks out of the door, Lena says, "You are a disgrace to your father's memory." She too prepares to leave.

Analysis

It becomes clearer that Walter's impulses are primarily class–motivated. After describing to his mother how he sees wealthy white men downtown, he expresses a very important principle that is at the crux of the formulation of his identity.

> MAMA Son–how come you talk so much 'bout money?
>
> WALTER *(With immense passion)* Because it is life, Mama!

In this statement, Hansberry reveals that Walter's dreams and aspirations are a perversion of the American dream. The American dream in its entirety upholds intangibles such as liberty, justice, and equality. Walter's version, however, has reduced this dream into the crude, materialistic desire for money. Walter has accepted a corrupt middle class ideology that places money and power above all else. As he is unable to achieve that which he most desires, a peculiar breed of bitterness begins to consume him. A major obstacle in Walter's path is racism. As an African–American male, Walter has been systematically disenfranchised from the American dream he so fervently praises. The system of racism has placed the white man's desire for economic power and elevated social status above the ideals of liberty, justice, and equality. Therefore, the very perversion of the American dream that Walter buys into is the same one that oppresses him.

Part of Walter's oppression is his emasculation. His subservient job as a chauffeur and his inability to provide adequately for his family all whittle away at his self–esteem. When Mama refuses to invest in the liquor store, Walter says,

> Well, *you* tell that to my boy tonight when you put him to sleep on the living–room couch...Yeah–and tell it to my wife, Mama, tomorrow when she has to go out of here to look after somebody else's kids. And tell it to *me*, Mama, every time we need a new pair of curtains and I have to watch *you* go out and work in somebody's kitchen.

Economic oppression hinders Walter's ability to fulfill his roles as a father, a husband, and a son. Up until now, Walter has "performed" these roles despite his inability to truly fulfill them. He plays his part well: when Travis asks for fifty cents, he gives his son a dollar even though he does not have enough money left to get to work.

However, when his wife tells him she is considering an abortion, Walter is no longer able to perform the role of the content husband. His mother expects him to be like his father.

> MAMA I'm waiting to hear how you be your father's son. Be the man he was...*(Pause. The silence shouts)* Your wife say she going to destroy your child. And I'm waiting to hear you talk like him and say we a people who give children life, not who destroys them–*(she rises)* I'm waiting to see you stand up and look like your daddy and say we done give up one baby to poverty and that we ain't going to give up nary another one...I'm waiting.
>
> WALTER Ruth– *(He can say nothing)*
>
> MAMA If you a son of mine, tell her! (WALTER *picks up his keys and his coat and walks out. She continues, bitterly*) You...You are a disgrace to your father's memory. Somebody get me my hat!

The world the Youngers live in stifles reproduction and forward motion. Walter is unable to provide for the physical needs of his unborn child, and is unable to reproduce the model of masculinity given to him by his father. Lena pushes her son to act like his father, but Walter is unable to do so. He falters under his mother's gaze, and must run away from her disapproving stare.

With such a brief play, Hansberry is able to address a remarkable number of issues pertinent to the African–American community. One issue dealt with in this scene is the relationship between African–Americans and Africa. Like many cultures who have experienced Diaspora, there is a disconnect between the native and displaced peoples. Mama represents the knowledge base of the majority of African–Americans about Africa at that time. She believes the image perpetuated by the media (which includes not only radio and television but also plays) about Africa. One misconception Beneatha brings up is about Africans not wearing clothes, like in *Tarzan*. Beneatha also addresses the danger of the church's "saving missions" to Africa. Beneatha explains how this paternalistic attitude is misdirected, and says that what Africa really needs is to be rescued from French and British imperialism.

Summary and Analysis of Act II scene i

Later on Saturday, the scene opens with Ruth ironing and Beneatha getting ready for a date that night. She has on the Nigerian dress that Asagai gave her earlier. Beneatha dances to Nigerian music as she shows off her African garb, and sings in a Nigerian dialect. Walter walks into the apartment drunk but instinctively starts dancing, loving the beat of the drum in the music. During this scene, the inebriated Walter begins to act out a scene in which he is the chief of a tribe. He prepares his imaginary tribe for war by invoking war songs and the songs of his ancestors.

Just as he makes his great speech, Walter is jerked back into reality, the stage lights turn back on, and George Murchison enters. Ruth, embarrassed, tells Walter (who has gotten on the table in his excitement) to get down and act properly. George, thoroughly confused, addresses Beneatha and asks her to change out of her "costume" and get ready for their theatre date. Beneatha, in a moment of indignation, removes her headdress and reveals to George Murchison her hair in its natural afro state. George is completely shocked. Beneatha seems to have expected this reaction and challenges George's discomfort with her natural hair, accusing him of being "an assimilationist Negro." Thus, the debate about the merits of their African heritage begins. George minimizes the importance of West African history and calls their heritage "nothing but a bunch of raggedy–assed spirituals and some grass huts!" Beneatha, highly insulted, asserts the importance of African history to civilization, citing the example of the surgical advances made by the Ashanti people.

Beneatha leaves George in the living room while she gets changed for their date. George, left to be entertained by Ruth and Walter, takes every opportunity to brag about how well–traveled he is. When asked what time the show starts, George says, "It's an eight–thirty curtain. That's just Chicago, though. In New York standard curtain time is 8:40." In order to save face, Walter pretends to have been to New York several times, and then begins to ridicule George about his collegiate dress. Walter, still inebriated, inquires about George's wealthy father, and then begins to tell George about his business plans. Insulted when George snubs him, Walter begins to challenge George in earnest. George dismisses Walter as bitter, and Walter responds, "And you–ain't you bitter, man?...Bitter? Man, I'm a volcano." Beneatha enters the scene again dressed in a cocktail dress but with her hair still natural. George and Beneatha get ready to leave, and as a final insult, George says to Walter, "Good night, Prometheus!" to highlight Walter's ignorance of Greek mythology.

With George and Beneatha gone, Walter turns his agitation towards his wife. Ruth offers Walter hot milk and coffee to help him with his hangover, but Walter complains that she does not give him what he really needs. He begins to ask Ruth about what has come between them, and why their relationship has changed.

Mama comes back home after having been gone all afternoon. Lena calls Travis to her and reveals to all of them that she has used the insurance money to put a down payment on a house. Ruth and Travis are excited; Walter remains silent. When Mama reveals that the address is 406 Clybourne Street, Clybourne Park, Walter voices his objection about moving into a white neighborhood. Mama explains that she did her best and tried to find the nicest house for the least amount of money. After sharing her news, Lena asks what Walter thinks. He ends the scene by stating,

> What you need me to say you done right for? You the head of this family. You run our lives like you want to. It was your money and you did what you wanted with it. So what you need me to say it was all right for?...so you butchered up a dream of mine–you–who always taking 'bout your children dreams...

Analysis

While the last scene focused on Asagai, George Murchison, his antithesis, is introduced in this scene. Whereas Asagai represents liberal idealism and progressive free thought, George Murchison represent the conservative bourgeoisie. The interaction between Walter and George reveals the tension between the working and upper–middle classes. Beneatha is excited about her newly obtained gifts from Asagai: a Nigerian robe and music. Having tried on the robe, Beneatha turns on the Nigerian music. Walter, drunk, walks in and almost instinctively starts dancing to the rhythm of the drums. On a conscious level, Walter is not necessarily receptive to Beneatha's afrocentric ideology. For example, Walter makes fun of Beneatha's hair when she wears it in an natural afro as opposed to straightened. In front of her guest, Walter laughing says, "Well, I'll be damned. So that's what they mean by the African bush." On a subconscious level, however, Walter acknowledges their common African heritage when he dances to the drumbeat. It is in the African setting that he is able to imagine his masculinity restored. In his imagination, he is a great chief and a descendant of royalty. However, George's arrival disrupts Walter's world, jarringly bringing him back to a reality where he is poor, working–class, and unable to provide for his family.

Education and class create a chasm between George and Walter. Walter's resentment of Beneatha's college education is demonstrated in his expressed desire for Beneatha to be a nurse in the play's first scene. That resentment resurfaces in his conversation with George. Intimidated by George's exposure and travels, Walter begins to attack George's attire.

> WALTER I(Looking MURCHISON over from head to toe, scrutinizing his carefully casual tweed sports jacket over cashmere V–neck sweater over soft eyelet shirt and tie, and soft slacks, finished off with white buckskin shoes)

Why all you college boys wear them faggoty–looking white shoes? Whereas in the beginning of the scene George ridicules Beneatha's Nigerian costume, now the tables are turned, and Walter ridicules George's bourgeoisie costume. In this conversation, he not only undercuts the value of his education, but also challenges his masculinity with the homosexual connotation of the word "faggoty." George returns the insult at the end of his visit by referring to Walter as "Prometheus" in an effort to highlight his ignorance.

Hansberry skillfully captures the intra–racial tensions in the African–American community. Because society often places blacks in a single, indistinct category, wealthy African–Americans try even harder to distinguish themselves from poor African–Americans. As illustrated in Ralph Ellison's *Invisible Man*, blacks in America are treated as if they are invisible and insignificant. The threat of being treated as such is imminent. Often, the difference between affluence and poverty within the black community is only a generation removed, and assimilation becomes a survival strategy in order to gain acceptance by the majority. George Murchison's collegiate dress is a prime example of how he attempts to use his clothes to set him apart from the uneducated working–class.

Summary and Analysis of Act II scene ii

On a Friday night a few weeks later, George and Beneatha come back to the apartment. George wants to kiss; Beneatha, however, wants to talk. George, frustrated, says to Beneatha, "You're a nice–looking girl…all over. That's all you need, honey, forget the atmosphere…I don't go out with you to discuss the nature of 'quiet desperation' or to hear all about your thoughts." Beneatha takes all this in and then asks George to leave. As he is leaving, Mama enters. Sensing the awkwardness, Mama asks what the matter is. Beneatha tells her, and for once Mama agrees with her daughter's assessment that she should not be bothered with George.

[The following scene with Ms. Johnson was cut from the original version of this play. Ms. Johnson, a nosy neighbor, has heard that the Youngers are moving. Under the pretense of offering the Youngers congratulations on the move and on Ruth's pregnancy, the woman comes over to cast doubt on their decision to move into a white neighborhood. Ms. Johnson happens to mention a recent newspaper article about a local Chicago family that moved into a white neighborhood and was bombed. After implying that Beneatha is uppity because she has a college education and that Walter ought to be satisfied as a chauffeur, Mrs. Johnson agrees to disagree with Lena and leaves.]

Ruth receives a call from Walter's boss's wife, Mrs. Arnold. Ruth discovers that Walter has not been at work for the past three days, and will lose his job if he does not show up soon. When Mama inquires where Walter has been, he confesses that on the first day he borrowed his friend Willy's car and drove into the country to look at steel mills, and then went to a local bar, the Green Hat. On the second day, he drove the car all the way up to Wisconsin to look at the farms, ending the day again at the Green Hat. Today, he says, he walked all over the South Side of Chicago, and plans to go right back to the Green Hat.

Mama realizes that her son is in a crisis and makes an important decision. She says, BLOCKQUOTE [There ain't nothing as precious to me…There ain't nothing worth holding on to, money dreams nothing else–if it means–if it means it's going to destroy my boy…I'm telling you to be the head of this family from now on like you suppose to be.] Lena then gives Walter the rest of the insurance money to invest as he pleases. After giving him $3,500 as a down payment, Mama gives the remaining $6,500 to Walter, asking only that he put aside $3000 for Beneatha's medical school education. Walter is amazed that his mother trusts him with the money. Travis enters the room, and Walter, excited about his new–found responsibility, tells his son about his hopes and dreams of working in a office, driving a nice car, having a nice house, and sending his son to college.

Analysis

Like many college students in their early twenties, Beneatha is searching for her identity. Through Beneatha's relationships, Hansberry makes a valid point that the type of person one chooses as a partner is just as much a statement of one's identity as the ideas and thoughts they profess with their own mouths. George reveals in this scene that even though he and Beneatha are being exposed to the same radical and enlightening ideas, he does not truly accept them as his own. He has probably learned about women's struggle for suffrage just as Beneatha has, but he still values a woman's physical attributes over the thoughts and ideas she has to offer. George says, "You're a nice–looking girl...all over. That's all you need, honey, forget the atmosphere...I don't go out with you to discuss the nature of 'quiet desperation' or to hear all about your thoughts."

The scene with Ms. Johnson was cut from the original production, yet the scene is significant because it reveals the feelings that other African–Americans might have had about the move. Ms. Johnson has dropped by uninvited to share her opinions. She feels that Beneatha has been acting snooty since she has started college, and believes that Walter should be satisfied as a chauffeur. Unable to withhold her comments any longer, Mama defends her son by saying,

> My husband always said being any kind of servant wasn't a fit thing for a man to have to be. He always said a man's hands was made to make things, or turn the earth with–not to drive nobody's car for 'em–or...carry they slop jars. And my boy is just like him–he wasn't meant to wait on nobody.

This speech is interesting because it reveals where Mama draws the line: one might expect that distinction between servants and those being served might be made along monetary lines, but Mama asserts that what gives a man honor is the act of creating, whether he is a carpenter or a farmer. Walter's liquor store hits the essence of this philosophy. Even though Lena may have moral objections to liquor, ultimately Walter's entrepreneurial spirit is what validates his dream in Mama's eyes.

Lena understands what is at stake when a man's dream is deferred. Even though Walter has been talking about his plans and dreams for so long that Ruth has begun to turn a deaf ear, Mama does not grasp the fragility of his state until Walter is unable to stand up like his father and demand that Ruth not have an abortion. Lena attempts to remedy the situation by making a down payment on the house. When Walter misses work, however, Lena realizes that the house is her dream – not Walter's. At the end of the first scene of the second act, Walter feels insignificant even while Ruth becomes elated at the news of the new house. He wanted to be the heroic provider, bringing redemption to his family. At this point Lena makes a very difficult decision, and gives him authority over the insurance money.

In this play, Hansberry makes a statement about black families and how they are driven to support one another unconditionally. Mama realizes that her attempt to fix the problem is insufficient. The money represents a transfer of power. Walter is now the head of the Younger household. For the first time, he is trusted to make critical decisions that affect not only himself, but his entire family. Even though both Ruth and Lena have reservations about the sustainability of his plans, they must follow his lead. At last, the scene when Walter pretended to be Chaka Zulu has become reality: he is now the leader of his family.

Summary and Analysis of Act II scene iii

The play continues one week later on moving day, a Saturday. The scene begins with Ruth singing, "I don't feel no ways tired" in a triumphant voice before the curtain rises. Ruth is alone in the living room when Beneatha enters with a guitar. Ruth is excited about their new house; she has bought new curtains, even though she does not know the window measurements. As Beneatha helps Ruth pack up and label the good china, Ruth excitedly says that she and her husband went on a date the night before, and that they held hands during the movie. Walter and Ruth's relationship, it seems, is flourishing.

The relationship between Beneatha and Walter also seems to be getting better. Walter enters the living room and dances with his wife, and then begins to playfully tease his sister about her new ideas, calling her "the chairman of the Committee on Unending Agitation" because she is always talking about race. Beneatha takes the teasing in stride and answers the doorbell.

A middle–aged white man in a business suit stands there, and declares that he is looking for Lena Younger. Since Mama is not home, Walter agrees to speak with the visitor. His name is Mr. Karl Lindner, and he is from the Clybourne Park Improvement Association. Walter invites him in and offers him something to drink, but Lindner declines. He introduces the association as a welcoming committee for people moving into the neighborhood. Lindner mentions the recent incidence of a bombing after a black family moved into a white neighborhood. In order to prevent this sort of deplorable event, Lindner and the association he represents want an open discussion where they can just "sit down and talk to each other." Lindner, it seems, does not want the family moving into the neighborhood. He explains,

> You've got to admit that a man, right or wrong, has the right to want to have the neighborhood he lives in a certain kind of way. And at the moment the overwhelming majority of our people out there feel that people get along better, take more of a common interest in the life of the community, when they share a common background. I want you to believe me when I tell you the race prejudice simply doesn't enter into it. It is a matter of the people of Clybourne Park believing, rightly or wrongly, as I say, that for the happiness of all concerned that our Negro families are happier when they live in their *own* communities.

The Association is willing to pay them more than their down payment if they will abandon their plans to move into the neighborhood. Beneatha, having suspected his intentions, is the first to react with sarcasm. Walter, taken aback, gathers his thoughts and tells the visitor to get out. Mr. Lindner, placing his business card on the table, leaves.

Mama returns with Travis, and the family tells her about Mr. Lindner's visit. Mama shakes her head in response. Beneatha cracks a joke to break the awkwardness, and then turns Mama's attention to her plant, asking if she is going to take that "raggedy–looking old thing." Lena, in mock imitation of her daughter's earlier statement, replies, "It expresses ME!" During this time, Walter, Ruth, and Beneatha present Mama with a gift of gardening tools. Young Travis is anxious to give his grandmother his own gift, an elaborate gardening hat. The rest of the family teases Travis for its lavishness, but Lena defends him and promptly put on the hat to show her approval.

The door bell rings: it is Bobo, visiting unexpectedly. Bobo is nervous and frightened, and wants to speak with Walter. Walter is excited to hear about how the business venture is going, as both Walter and Bobo gave Willy their share of the money to invest in the liquor store. Although Walter could not make it to the meeting, Willy and Bobo were to meet at the train station in order to go to Springfield. In Springfield, they would obtain the liquor license necessary to proceed. Bobo, however, says that Willy never arrived. Walter learns that he has been scammed out of his father's insurance money. No money has been put away for Beneatha's medical school: he has invested all of the $6,500 Lena gave him in the store. Walter, in a moment of despair, cries out, "THAT MONEY IS MADE OUT OF MY FATHER'S FLESH." Walter must now tell his family the news. Upon learning of her brother's deception, Beneatha cries out in rage. Mama is devastated, remembering how her husband worked himself to his death. The scene closes with Lena looking to heaven for strength.

Analysis

The title of the play comes from a phrase in Langston Hughes's poem "Harlem." The poem's images beautifully capture the tensions between life and death, hope and despair, and destruction and fulfillment. Hansberry could have chosen numerous images to represent these themes. In fact, a draft version of the play was named *The Crystal Stair* – an image borrowed from Langston Hughes's poem by the same title. The raisin, however, is particularly significant to the themes of salvation and fertility. Hansberry paints a landscape of poverty that is in itself a wasteland: dry, desolate, and infertile. Walter works, but is unable to provide for his family. Ruth considers abortion because the family cannot support another life. Even Walter's dreams falls on deaf ears. In the midst of this spiritual drought, Walter seeks refuge in the bar the Green Hat: a mirage that offers false refuge through a liquid that cannot hydrate the body or the soul.

On the surface, it may appear that regeneration comes to Walter through the insurance money. The scene opens with the family packing, a silent action that symbolically speaks volumes about the family's potential for growth and mobility. The relationship between Walter and Ruth is budding once again: they go out on a date, hold hands, and dance romantically in the living room (all activities emblematic of youth). Walter and Beneatha's arguments are filled with youthful teasing, rather anger and resentment, and when an obstacle rears its ugly head in the form of Mr. Lindner, Walter easily finds the inner strength to resist the temptation. By the end of the scene, however, defeat comes from within. Walter has trusted his friend Willy Harris without question to invest in the liquor store, and finds himself betrayed. It is a harsh reminder to the dreamer that greed and self–interest still do exist. By the end of the scene, the insurance money proves to have been a false savior.

Hansberry's play is timeless because she is able to make the political realm symbiotic with the very art of the stage. The audience is drawn into a conversation that forces them to unite the idea of poverty with its reality. The appearance of Mr. Lindner on stage is the physical manifestation of the housing controversy that has been a looming presence throughout the play, giving a voice to the roaches and rats that encroach upon the very livelihood of the Youngers. Mr. Lindner is the only white man who appears in the play. He not only represents the Clybourne Park Improvement Association, but also the attitude of many white people of that time. He speaks to imminent danger and the hypocrisy that surrounds the issue of integration. Lindner says, "I am sure you people must be aware of some of the incidents which have happened in various parts of the city when colored people have moved into the area." The address of "you people" immediately draws a distinction between the Youngers and Mr. Lindner, between "them" and "us", and between black and white. And even though he goes on to denounce such violent action, the very mention of the occurrence places the threat on the table. He continues to insist that people get along when they share "a common interest" and "that racial prejudice simply doesn't enter into it." Lindner uses the rhetoric of equality, but perverts it to justify a system that reinforces inequality. Through these words, the audience realizes that even though equality is inscribed in the Constitution, it is not yet ingrained in the heart of man. Lindner's words echo like empty rhetoric that is both contradictory and self–serving but, ultimately lies at the heart of many civil rights issues today.

Summary and Analysis of Act III

One hour after Bobo's visit, the Younger home is silent and sullen. The lighting is gloomy and gray. Walter lies dismally on his bed while his sister, Beneatha, sits at the living room table. Asagai happens to drop by: unaware of the recent turn of events, he is genuinely happy and excited about the Youngers' move. Before he is able to get started on a diatribe about movement and progress, Beneatha informs Asagai that Walter has lost the insurance money.

Realizing the gravity of the situation, Asagai asks Beneatha how she is doing. Beneatha, it appears, has lost hope. For the first time, the audience learns why she wants to become a doctor. Beneath recalls sledding on ice–covered steps in the winter time when a young boy named Rufus fell off his sled and severely injured his head. As the young boy got into the ambulance, Beneatha believed that he was beyond repair, but the next time she saw him he only has a small line down his face. Beneatha became fascinated by the concrete manner in which a doctor can identify a problem and fix it. Now, after recent events, Beneatha has lost sight of her childhood motivation, and believes that medicine is not enough to solve society's problems. She says, "What about all the and thieves and just plain idiots who will come into power and steal and plunder the same as before." Beneatha feels as if true progress is unattainable, and that her fate is not within her own control.

Asagai stays true to his idealism and belief in progress. He talks about how he still has hope for his people in Africa, no matter how many setbacks they may encounter. He encourages Beneatha to stop dwelling on the past and think about her future. Giving her hope once again, Asagai surprises Beneatha by asking her to come to Nigeria with him and practice medicine there. Surprised, she refuses to give him an answer immediately.

Walter enters, and Beneatha immediately hurls sarcastic epithets at him, such as "Symbol of the Rising Class" and "Titan of the System". Walter leaves without responding to his sister. Meanwhile, Ruth and Mama are trying to figure out what to do – whether to continue on with the move, or to cancel the appointment with the moving men, who are scheduled to arrive shortly. Reflecting on how people in her past always told her that her ideas were too big, Mama feels ready to give up. She is already planning how they can make their present apartment more pleasant. Ruth, however, is insistent that the family should continue with the move. Ruth pleads,

> Lena–I'll work…I'll work twenty hours a day in all the kitchens in Chicago…I'll strap my baby on my back if I have to and scrub all the floors in America and wash all the sheets in America if I have to– but we got to MOVE! We got to get OUT OF HERE!

Walter comes back from his errand, having decided upon a plan of action. He has decided to accept Mr. Lindner's offer to buy the house from the Youngers for more than they paid. The family is horrified at his decision, but Walter is tired of being taken advantage of. He is tired of being concerned about right or wrong, when other people are getting ahead. Lena tries to reason with her son. She says, "Son–I cane from five generations of people who was slaves and sharecroppers–but ain't nobody in my family never let nobody pay 'em no money that was a way of telling us we wasn't fit to walk the earth." Walter's mind, however, is made up. He feels that he deserves to have nice things, and believes that doing business with Mr. Lindner is just a means to an end. Beneatha is furious, and disowns Walter as her brother. Mama confronts Beneatha about her words and insists that it is during Walter's lowest moments that he needs his family's love and support the most.

Mr. Lindner and the moving men arrive simultaneously. Ruth motions for Travis to go downstairs while Walter deals with Mr. Lindner, but Mama insists that Travis stay right there and witness the actions of his father. Under the innocent gaze of his son, Walter is unable to make the deal with Mr. Lindner, and tells him, "We don't want your money." The moment is truly heroic, and marks Walter's introduction into manhood. The family, triumphant, bustles into action as they continue with their move. As the family gathers their things together, Beneatha announces her decision to become a doctor in Africa. Walter retorts that she should be concerned about marrying a wealthy man like George Murchison. Beneatha is furious, and they begin to argue just as they did at the beginning of the play. Everyone but Mama exits the stage. Making sure to bring her plant with her, Mama takes a last look at the apartment before leaving it forever.

Analysis

Walter's nihilism manifests when his dreams dissipate before his eyes. He says,

> Mama, you know it's all divided up. Life is. Sure enough. Between the takers and the "tooken." *(He laughs.)* I've figured it out finally. *(He looks around at them.)* Yeah. Some of us always getting "token." *(He laughs.)* And you know why the rest of us do? 'Cause we all mixed up. Mixed up bad. We get to looking 'round for the right and the wrong; and we worry about it and cry about it and stay up night trying to figure out 'bout the wrong and right of things all the time...And all the time, man, them takers is out there operating, just taking and taking."

Several events provoke Walter's reaction. Walter, having been mocked by misfortune, feels as if his autonomy has been lost and his manhood has been slighted once again.

Beneatha's idealism breaks down as she grapples with her brother's failure and its effect on her future. Asagai appears at Beneatha's most desperate moment, offering words of hope. He is able to use his knowledge of Africa's struggle for independence to provide her with encouragement, even while Walter struggles for his own autonomy. Through Asagai, Hansberry is able to connect the significance of global events to the individual. Some critics point out that Beneatha's relationship with Asagai (and thus her perception of Africa) is romanticized. Unlike Walter, whose dreams and ideas are seriously challenged within the scope of the play, Asagai's idealism remains pure and untainted. Critic C.W.E. Bigsby notes that Asagai is like an "oracle whose declarations make sense only to those who are to the stereotype African…rich in wisdom and standing, like the noble savage, as a reminder of primal innocence." At this moment, however, Asagai's idealist vision is the nourishment "Alaiyo" needs.

With the loss of the money, the entire family must face dreams that are deferred once again, and each one reacts differently. Walter and Beneatha are not the only ones who feel like giving up. Mama abandons hope, telling her children to unpack and to cancel the moving men. She says, "Lord, ever since I was a little girl I always remember people saying, 'Lena–Lena Eggleston, you aims too high all the time. You needs to slow down and see life a little more like it is. Just slow down some.' That's what they always used to say down home–'Lord, that Lena Eggleston is a high–minded thing. She'll get her due one day!'" Mama feels as if the unfortunate loss of the insurance money is due punishment for having high expectations. She has accepted her lot in life, and is already planning how to spruce up the apartment. Ruth is the one person who is unwilling to let go of her dream so easily. When Lena gives up and begins making preparations to stay, Ruth insists, "We got to MOVE! We got to get OUT OF HERE!!" She is willing to work several jobs in order to make the move possible.

Even though their goals are very different in nature, the insurance money from Walter Sr. is the catalyst for each of their dreams. The $10,000 offers the Youngers the ability to achieve salvation: Mama will get her dream home, Beneatha her medical education, and Walter his liquor store. However, the money comes at a price: Walter Sr. must die for the Youngers to have any chance of getting out of their futile situation. In many ways, the insurance money acts as a *deus ex machina*. The term is used in reference to a trope in ancient Greek plays when a character doomed to die is miraculously saved from destruction. At first glance the fortunate and unfortunate ways in which the money comes in and goes out of the Younger household add absurdity to a play where circumstance and fate seems to overpower human autonomy. However, Hansberry complicates this assumption by making Walter's decision to choose dignity rather than submission the true means to salvation.

Suggested Essay Questions

1. The American dream means something different to each character in *A Raisin in the Sun*. Discuss these differences and how they conflict with one another.
2. Lorraine Hansberry is often viewed as a visionary because of her ability to predict many of the relevant issues to the African–American community today. Identify some of these issues and explain how they are the same or different from how Hansberry portrayed them.
3. Within the Younger household, there are three generations of women. Compare and contrast how the characters each form their unique identities.
4. Critical reception to *A Raisin in the Sun* was not all positive when the play first came out. One of the major points of contention was that the play was pro–integration. Some segments of the African–American community felt that integration actually was not the end–all answer to America's race problem. Discuss the ways in which the idea of integration is presented throughout the play. Is Hansberry's presentation one–sided, or does she raise issues relevant to both viewpoints?
5. Although Travis does not have many lines, his character is significant. Discuss Travis' importance to some of the prominent themes throughout the play.
6. Discuss how the Youngers' environment impacts their life.
7. In 1959, abortion was a taboo topic. Discuss how the issue is presented in the play, and how the audience might have reacted.
8. How do you think Lorraine Hansberry's own life influenced *A Raisin in the Sun*?
9. Many critics assert that the art of Hansberry's play is that it is less about race than about humanity. Do you think the play would be equally compelling if the actors were white, or some other minority group? Explain why or why not.
10. Even though Walter Sr. never appears in the play, he is an important character. Discuss his significance.

"Harlem" by Langston Hughes

What happens to a dream deferred?

Does it dry up

Like a raisin in the sun?

Or fester like a sore–

And then run?

Does it stink like rotten meat?

Or crust and sugar over–

Like a syrupy sweet?

Maybe it just sags

Like a heavy load.

Or does it explode?

Housing Discrimination

Hansberry's play is timeless because she is able to make contemporary political issues part of the very art of the stage, drawing her audience into a conversation that continues to be relevant even today. The appearance of Mr. Lindner on stage is the physical manifestation of the housing controversy that has been a menacing presence throughout the play. Housing has various implications not only for health, but also for education. Although the burden fell most heavily upon African–Americans, they were not the only ethnic group affected by housing discrimination during this era. Restrictive covenants also prohibited Italians, Asians, and Jews from residing in certain areas. The Housing Act of 1949 had only been in place for ten years when the play hit the stage, but the majority of African Americans were still living in poverty. The law suggests that integrated neighborhoods will benefit from improved health and living standards, as well as from the growth and advancement of under–served communities. However, several practices continued even after the passing of the act that made integration difficult. Real estate agents would sell houses at an inflated cost after having coerced the white owners into selling at a loss because of the threat of integration. Rental agencies would delay appointments with African–Americans in hopes that a white customer would rent first. The Fair Housing Policy of 1968 attempted to address the problem by forbidding these deceptive practices. Even today, housing continues to be issue, particularly given how it affects education. Schools are still funded through property taxes in most area, and children have the option of attending alternate schools through busing or school vouchers to private institutions.

Author of ClassicNote and Sources

Cheryl Sherrod, author of ClassicNote. Completed on April 29, 2006, copyright held by GradeSaver.

Updated and revised Jordan Berkow June 15, 2006. Copyright held by GradeSaver.

Cheney, Anne. Lorraine Hansberry. New York: Twayne Publishers, 1994.

Domina, Lynn. Understanding A Raisin in the Sun: A Student Casebook to Issues, Sources, and Historical Documents. Westport, Connecticut: Greenwood Press, 1998.

Hansberry, Lorraine. A Raisin in the Sun. New York: Vintage Books, 1994.

Scheader, Catherine. Lorraine Hansberry: Playwright and Voice of Justice. Berkeley Heights, NJ: Enslow Publishers, Inc., 1998.

Abramson, Doris E. "The Fifties." Negro Playwrights in American Theatre, 1925–59. Columbia University Pr. 1969. 165–266. Rpt. in Contemporary Literary Criticism. Ed. Roger Matuz. Vol. 62. Detroit: Gale, 1991.

Baraka, Amiri. "A Raisin in the Sun's Enduring Passion." A Raisin in the Sun and The Sign in Sidney Brustein's Window. Ed. Robert Nemiroff. New York: New American Library, 1987. 9–20.

Bigsby, C.W. E. "Lorraine Hansberry." Confrontation and Commitment: A Study of Contemporary American Drama, 1959–66. University of Missouri Pr. 1968. 156–73. Rpt. in Contemporary Literary Criticism. Ed. Roger Matuz. Vol. 62. Detroit: Gale, 1991.

Brown, Lioyd W/. "Lorraine Hansberry as Ironist: A Repraisal of 'A Raisin in the Sun'." The Journal of Black Studies. Vol. 4, No.3, March 1974. 237–247. Rpt. in Contemporary Literary Criticism. Ed. Roger Matuz. Vol. 62. Detroit: Gale, 1991.

Cruse, Harold. "Lorraine Hansberry." The Crisis of the Negro Intellectual. William Morrow &Company, Inc. 1967. 267–84. Rpt. in Contemporary Literary Criticism. Ed. Roger Matuz. Vol. 62. Detroit: Gale, 1991.

"Lorraine Hansberry" Contemporary Literary Criticism. Ed. Roger Matuz. Vol. 62. Detroit: Gale, 1991.

Morton–Mollo, Sherry. "Lorraine Hansberry." Great American Writers Twentieth Century. Ed. R. Baird Shuman. New York: Marshall Cavendish, 2002.

Nemiroff, Robert. "Introduction." A Raisin in the Sun. New York: Vintage Books,

1994.

Short, Hugh. "Hansberry, Lorraine." Critical Survey of Drama: Second Revised Edition. Ed. Maria Irene Fornes and Tina Howe. Vol. 3. Pasedena, Ca: Salem Press, Inc., 2003.

Hansberry, Lorraine. "Willy Loman, Walter younger, and He Who Must Live." The Village Voice. Vol IV, No. 42, August 12, 1959. 7–8. Rpt. in Contemporary Literary Criticism. Ed. Roger Matuz. Vol. 62. Detroit: Gale, 1991.

Essay: The Aspirations of Women in A Raisin in the Sun

by Emilie Browne
March 22, 2003

Lorraine Hansberry's A Raisin in the Sun challenges the stereotype of 1950's America as a country full of doting, content housewives. The women in this play, Mama, Ruth and Beneatha, represent three generations of black women who, despite their double fronted subordination, continue to dream of a better tomorrow. Although the aspirations of these women differ in subject, they all involve the furthering their roles as women, whether it be owning a house, paying for a child's education or attending Medical School.

For the Younger women, their dreams seem farther away than they would in the present for most females. Today, owning a house, paying for a child's education or gaining admittance to medical school is much more accessible than it was for these women. In the time this play is set, being a woman means marrying young, having a low desire for higher education and keeping a house clean for the male provider. Since the majority of this play centers around Walter Lee's struggles to prove his self–worth, it is easy to overlook thought–provoking Hansberry's portrayal of women. As a writer, Hansberry is ahead of her time, challenging an American society that is generally happy to leave women in the kitchen.

It seems that each the Younger women possess a certain advantage over Walter Lee. His aspirations involve schemes of making money fast. Walter Lee becomes so obsessed with financial wealth that he equates money to be the solution to all life's problems. As the play progresses, Walter becomes so out of touch with reality that he separates himself from his family because of his fluctuating moods. While Walter Lee is lost in bouts of elation and depression, it is the women in the family who must try and keep the family together.

Mama, Ruth and Beneatha all have very different perceptions of what it means to be a woman, resulting from their generation gap and individual experiences. Mama, the ruler of the family, takes a conservative view of the roles of women. A Christian woman who values moral accountability, she tries to keep her family from sacrificing their ethics in order to achieve. It is Mama who has the power of deciding how her husbands ten thousand dollar life insurance cheque that the other members of the family have been anticipating will be spent. As the Matriarch of the family, Mama always seems to have the best interests of the others in mind. A warm, supporting character who dreams of a nice house for her family to enjoy, Mama represents the ideal mother, bringing life to the nurturing side of women.

Ruth is a woman who is fairly neutral when it comes to the way she perceives her role as a woman. Not as conservative as Mama and hardly as radical as Beneatha,

Ruth represents a neutral force in the Younger house. It is apparent from Ruth's appearance that times have been hard on her, as she wears a tired expression. Ruth carries out the traditional domestic work of a woman, supplementing Walter Lee's income as a chauffeur by working as a cook and housekeeper for other families. Ruth shares Mama's enthusiasm for using the insurance money in order to secure a house of their own where she can spend as much time in the bathtub relaxing as she wants. Ruth is confronted with many internal conflicts when she discovers she is pregnant. Her relationship with Walter is becoming increasingly distant as proven when Walter finds out that Ruth is going to have a dangerous, illegal abortion and her husband responds "No–no–Ruth wouldn't do that." (75) This occurrence proves that Ruth and Walter Lee are at the point that although married, they don't really know each other anymore. Living in such impoverished conditions has left Ruth's maternal instinct in such a state of hopelessness that she would rather abort her child than raise it in such an environment where she wouldn't be able to provide for all of its needs.

Beneatha is the youngest and most radical of the Younger women. In A Raisin in the Sun, Beneatha represents what we today call a feminist. There is much tension between Beneatha and her older brother Walter, which mostly stems from the fact that Beneatha aspires to one day become a doctor. Walter is jealous of Beneatha's education and cannot understand why she would want to become a physician and would not "Go be a nurse like other women." (38) This shows that Walter is not comfortable with a woman having a higher level of education than he and that he has old fashioned ideas of what women should and should not be. As a young woman of twenty trying to find her identity, Beneatha experiments with many different forms of self–expression which expands to all aspects of her life, including the men she dates. George Murchison and Joseph Asagai are very different men from polar ends of the social spectrum. Both are African men with different viewpoints on life. Asagai, a Nigerian, represents a connection to Beneatha's heritage. Murchison, on the other hand, represents a black population who has been absorbed into the American culture, living for what has now been deemed the "American Dream." While Murchison has what Walter dreams of: financial security, a good education and a large home, Beneatha has more rapport with Asagai as it is he who is more down to earth, is familiar the struggles of Africans and wants to further his country much in the same way Beneatha dreams of furthering herself with a medical degree. In this way, Beneatha and Joseph are quite similar as they are looking for ways to free themselves from oppression in a world that does not yet know the value of diversity or respect for the differences of race and gender.

A Raisin in the Sun was written in a time where it "presaged the revolution in black and women's consciousness." (Nemiroff 5) Through Hansberry's characters motivations and actions, it is evident that a revolution is dawning in American society. An advent of social awakening is occurring, resulting from a climaxing unrest that could no longer be ignored, especially by the minorities whom it afflicted most. Through the women in this play, we are able to vicariously live a day in the life of black women and catch a glimpse of both the hardships and triumphs of their existence. Hansberry's mundane portrayal of these lives challenges the traditional views of womanhood by demonstrating that women are just as strong as men in hard situations and can continue to dream and challenge themselves despite the obstacles they encounter along the pathways of life.

Essay: Viewing the World from Different Angles: Generation Gaps in Hansberry's A Raisin in the Sun

by Kathryn Larrivee
January 01, 1995

The African–American experience of growing up in America changed dramatically throughout the course of the twentieth century, thus leading to differing views between the older and younger generations. In Lorraine Hansberry's play, A Raisin in the Sun, the character of Mama was raised during a point in time when racial prejudice was prevalent and blacks had virtually no opportunity to live out their dreams. On the other hand, her children, Walter and Beneatha, and her daughter–in–law, Ruth, grow up in a world where slavery exists only in history books, and although they still face financial hardship and racial discrimination, it is possible for blacks to become successful business men or even doctors. The younger generation's concept of the American dream reflects the changing times and the new opportunities that are now available for African–Americans. As a result of this generation gap, Mama and her children view the issues of religion, career choice, and abortion from extremely different angles, leading to much tension and anger in their relationship.

By viewing the dreams of Mama in comparison to the dreams of her children, one can clearly see the generation gap that exists between them. As a result of the changing times, Mama's dreams differ extremely from those of her children. She grew up in a time of much oppression and hardship – a time when she was unable to live out the simplest of dreams. All Mama ever wanted was a house with "a little garden in the back" (1209). After all, back then it was the most an African–American could hope for. During the 1960s however, it is much more common for an African–American to own a house, and since Walter grows up with this possibility, owning a house is not a high goal to set for himself. Instead, he sets his sights on a much more elaborate dream than his mother, in particular, being a successful businessman able to "pull [a] car up on the driveway" where his "gardener will be clipping away at the hedges" (1239–1240). Mama disapproves of Walter's dream, for she believes that they are not "business people," but rather "just plain working folks" (1208). She does not realize that nowadays African–Americans have more opportunities than she had growing up, and that, according to Walter, "colored people [are not] going to start getting ahead [until] they start gambling on some different kinds of things in the world, [such as] investments" (1208). Normally it would not be a problem for a grown man to make an investment that his mother does not approve of. However, Mama has the ten thousand dollars from her husband's insurance money that Walter needs in order to start his business. Because Mama does not agree with her son's choice to become a businessman, more specifically an owner of a liquor store, she refuses to give him the money. After Walter finds out that his mother spent the money on a down–payment for a house, thus fulfilling her own dream, he becomes enraged. When Mama wishes for Walter to tell her that he believes she did the right thing, he insults her:

What you need me to say you done right for? . . . It was your money and you did what you wanted with it. So you butchered up a dream of mine – you – who always talking 'bout your children's dreams . . . (1233).

Thus, because of their differing views on how the money should be spent, Walter and Mama are constantly at odds with one another.

Mama's disapproval does not stop with Walter's decision to invest in a liquor store, but continues with Ruth's decision to have an abortion. Mama has lived in poverty for her entire life, and it is because of this poverty that she lost her baby, "little Claude" (1209). She believes that "[they] are . . . people who give children life, not . . . destroy [it]" (1223). Ruth, however, has had the opportunity to raise a healthy son, and since she has never known any other way, she takes this for granted. Ruth does not view her unborn child as part of the family, and thus when determining what is in her family's best interest, she fails to think of the baby. Ruth comes to the conclusion that bringing another child into their already crowded apartment would be unfair to her family. Mama, on the other hand, is grateful for being able to have the opportunity to give birth to a healthy baby, since she knows that at the time many African–American babies were dying from poverty, and just a short time before, from slavery. It is because of this that she strongly disagrees with Ruth's decision to have an abortion. Mama does not understand how a woman who has the opportunity to give birth to a child would even think "about getting rid of [it]" (1223). When she informs Walter of Ruth's decision, he is unable to say anything to his wife and leaves the room. Mama angrily yells after him, "If you a son of mine, tell her [not to have the abortion]! You . . . you are a disgrace to your father's memory" (1223). By reading this quote, one can see that more tension arises in Walter and Mama's relationship as a result of her strong stance on the issue of abortion.

Mama also disapproves with the fact that Beneatha no longer believes in God. Beneatha constantly takes for granted the life that she is living, and when good fortune comes her way, such as the opportunity to become a doctor, she believes that it is commonplace, and therefore nothing to be thankful for. Mama, on the other hand, grew up in a time when good fortune was hard to come by. Whenever she is having a rough time, she places her faith in God and prays that everything will turn out all right. For example, when Walter loses the money for his sister's schooling, Mama asks God to "Look down here . . . and show [her] the strength" (1250). The issue of religion causes many arguments to occur between Beneatha and Mama, due to their different views. Beneatha, despite knowing that her mother is a religious woman, insists that "there simply is no blasted God – there is only man and it is he who makes miracles" (1212). Mama, deeply offended and disappointed in her daughter, is unable to control her anger. She slaps Beneatha across the face and insists she repeat the phrase "In my mother's house there is still God" (1212). In addition to this, Beneatha often uses the Lord's name in vain, thus further upsetting her mother. This constant conflict eventually takes its toll on their relationship, leaving them to feel bitterness and discomfort toward one another.

Throughout the course of the twentieth century, the concept of the American dream changed dramatically, as displayed in Lorraine Hansberry's play, A Raisin in the Sun. Through reading the play, one can tell that a generation gap exists between Mama and her children, for they view the world from extremely different angles. Their clashing views on the issues of religion, career choice, and abortion lead to many arguments between them, and as a result, their relationship is characterized by resentment and tension.

Works Cited

Hansberry, Lorraine. "A Raisin in the Sun." Literature: Reading Fiction, Poetry, and Drama. Compact ed. Ed. Robert DiYanni. New York: McGraw–Hill, 2000. 1198–1260

Quiz 1

1. **When did A Raisin in the Sun open on Broadway?**
   A. 1954
   B. 1959
   C. 1963
   D. 1975

2. **Which of the following is NOT a drama written by Lorraine Hansberry?**
   A. The Sign in Sidney Brustein's Window
   B. Les Blancs
   C. Les Negres
   D. The Drinking Gourd

3. **Lorraine Hansberry was the first African–American and the first woman to win:**
   A. a Grammy
   B. the Drama Circles Critics Award
   C. a Tony Award
   D. the Drama Desk Award

4. **Which of the following plays were NOT being run on Broadway while A Raisin in the Sun was playing?**
   A. Arthur Miller's The Crucible
   B. Archibald MacLeish's J. B.
   C. Eugene O' Neill's A Touch of the Poet
   D. Tennessee Williams' Sweet Bird of Youth

5. **How much is the insurance check for?**
   A. $8,000
   B. $10,000
   C. $11,000
   D. $15,000

6. **How many people live in the Younger apartment?**
   A. 3
   B. 4
   C. 5
   D. 7

7. **Where does the play take place?**
    A. Philadelphia
    B. Chicago
    C. Detroit
    D. Baltimore

8. **Walter is:**
    A. a waiter
    B. a chauffeur
    C. a cook
    D. a garbage man

9. **Walter wishes to invest the check in:**
    A. a liquor store
    B. a dry cleaning business
    C. a construction company
    D. a restaurant

10. **Mama objects to Walter's investment idea because:**
    A. her husband did not want the money invested
    B. of her religious convictions
    C. they have tried to invest in the business before and failed
    D. she does not want to spend the money but rather put it in a savings account

11. **Beneatha is:**
    A. a nurse
    B. medical student
    C. a college student
    D. unemployed

12. **Ruth is:**
    A. a nanny
    B. a teacher
    C. a cleaning woman
    D. a cook

13. **How many bedroom(s) does the apartment actually have?**

A. 0
B. 1
C. 2
D. 3

14. **Where does Travis sleep?**

A. in his bedroom
B. with his grandmother
C. with his parents
D. on the living room couch

15. **With whom do the Youngers share their bathroom?**

A. the Murchisons
B. no one
C. the Johnsons
D. Asagai

16. **Why does Travis ask for fifty cents?**

A. He needs it for school
B. He needs cab fare
C. He needs it to buy lunch
D. He wants a toy

17. **How much money does Walter give his son?**

A. a dollar
B. none
C. twenty–five cents
D. fifty cents

18. **What does Ruth prepare for Walter's breakfast?**

A. cereal
B. scrambled eggs
C. bacon and toast
D. poached eggs

19. **Why does Mama slap Beneatha?**
    A. Beneatha is pregnant
    B. Beneatha says there is no God
    C. Beneatha is dating Agasai
    D. Beneatha refuses to marry wealthy George Murchison

20. **Why does Ruth faint?**
    A. She is diabetic
    B. She is pregnant
    C. She does not want to go to work
    D. She is not eating properly

21. **Who sleeps in the converted "breakfast nook"?**
    A. Walter and Ruth
    B. Mama and Beneatha
    C. Ruth and Beneatha
    D. Walter and Beneatha

22. **What day of the week is the check supposed to arrive?**
    A. Friday
    B. Monday
    C. Saturday
    D. Wednesday

23. **Ruth is thinking about:**
    A. changing jobs
    B. quitting her job
    C. aborting her pregnancy
    D. hiring help for Mama

24. **Who brings in the insurance check?**
    A. Walter
    B. Travis
    C. Beneatha
    D. Ruth

25. **What does Agasai bring Beneatha back from Africa?**

A. a wedding ring

B. a necklace and a staue

C. his family

D. a Nigerian robe and African music

Quiz 1 Answer Key

1. **(B)** 1959
2. **(C)** Les Negres
3. **(B)** the Drama Circles Critics Award
4. **(A)** Arthur Miller's The Crucible
5. **(B)** $10,000
6. **(C)** 5
7. **(B)** Chicago
8. **(B)** a chauffeur
9. **(A)** a liquor store
10. **(B)** of her religious convictions
11. **(C)** a college student
12. **(C)** a cleaning woman
13. **(B)** 1
14. **(D)** on the living room couch
15. **(C)** the Johnsons
16. **(A)** He needs it for school
17. **(A)** a dollar
18. **(B)** scrambled eggs
19. **(B)** Beneatha says there is no God
20. **(B)** She is pregnant
21. **(A)** Walter and Ruth
22. **(C)** Saturday
23. **(C)** aborting her pregnancy
24. **(B)** Travis
25. **(D)** a Nigerian robe and African music

Quiz 2

1. **Where is Agasai from?**
    A. Liberia
    B. Nigeria
    C. Ethiopia
    D. South Africa

2. **Why does Mama not want Agasai to come by?**
    A. Mama does not like him
    B. The house is not clean
    C. Mama wants Beneatha to marry George
    D. He is African

3. **The word(s) Asagai uses to refer to Beneatha's straightened hair is:**
    A. "Uncle Tom"
    B. "exquisite"
    C. "assimilationist"
    D. "eurocentric"

4. **One of the misconceptions about African culture Beneatha does not warn Mama about is (are):**
    A. the effects of colonialism
    B. the pronunciation of Asagai's name
    C. confusing Liberia with Nigeria
    D. the untruths about Tarzan

5. **How old is Beneatha?**
    A. 18
    B. 19
    C. 20
    D. 21

6. **What name means "the one for whom bread is not enough?"**
    A. Alaiyo
    B. Yetunde
    C. Tokunbo
    D. Chioma

7. **Who says "WILL SOMEBODY PLEASE LISTEN TO ME TODAY?"**
   A. Walter
   B. Travis
   C. Beneatha
   D. Mama

8. **What do Travis and his friends chase?**
   A. a car
   B. a cat
   C. a dog
   D. a rat

9. **When Beneatha meets Asagai, what is she looking for?**
   A. her history class
   B. her glasses
   C. her identity
   D. her soulmate

10. **What is the primary reason Mama gives charitably to African missionary programs?**
   A. to feed the poor
   B. to save Africans from colonial powers
   C. to boost her own ego
   D. to save Africans from heathanism

11. **Which of the following episodes was NOT included in the original production?**
   A. Walter refusing to accept Lindner's offer
   B. Travis chasing a rat when playing with his friends
   C. Ruth waking Travis up for school
   D. Mama slapping Beneatha for not believing in God

12. **What does Mama want to invest the money in?**
   A. a dry–cleaning store
   B. a liquor store
   C. a trip to Europe
   D. Beneatha's medical school tuition and a house

13. **How many months pregnant is Ruth?**
   A. 2
   B. 4
   C. 5
   D. less than 1

14. **What does Mama ask to borrow from Ms Johnson?**
   A. kitchen cleanser
   B. milk
   C. baking soda
   D. sugar

15. **Why does George call Walter Lee Prometheus?**
   A. It demonstrates Walter's lack of knowledge
   B. Walter is inspired by the myth
   C. It is his nickname
   D. Because he likes inventing names

16. **Why does George object to Beneatha when he arrives to pick her up for their date?**
   A. The music is too loud
   B. Beneatha is wearing clothes another man bought for her
   C. Walter is drunk
   D. Her hair is natural

17. **In this play, "assimilation" means:**
   A. coming to terms with one's African heritage
   B. wanting to discard one's African past in order to gain acceptance amongst the white majority
   C. wanting to be prosperous
   D. being similar to two apparently different cultures

18. **When George arrives, Beneatha and Walter are:**
   A. in an argument
   B. dancing
   C. relieved that he has arrived
   D. drunk

19. **What idea(s) does Walter tell George about?**
A. the liquor store
B. the dry–cleaning business
C. all of the above

20. **What field does Beneatha inform George that the Ashanti have contributed to?**
A. architecture
B. warfare
C. surgery
D. sculpture

21. **Which item is not part of George's ensemble?**
A. tweed sports jacket
B. white buckskin shoes
C. glasses
D. V–neck cashmere sweater

22. **When Ruth reveals to Walter that she is pregnant, what is his reaction?**
A. He encourages her not to have the baby
B. He decides to forgo his business plans in favor of getting a bigger house
C. He is excited to welcome another member to the family
D. He gets drunk

23. **When Mama returns from having been gone all day, what news does she have for the family?**
A. She has paid Beneatha's medical education in full
B. She has placed a down payment on a new house
C. She has bought the family a car
D. She has bought several items for the new baby

24. **Why is the family hesistant about Mama's purchase?**
A. The house is in a white neighborhood
B. The house is in a Jewish neighborhood
C. The house is dilapidated
D. The house is in the ghetto

25. **The Youngers are:**

A. Jewish
B. Nigerian
C. African–American
D. Caucasian

Quiz 2 Answer Key

1. **(B)** Nigeria
2. **(B)** The house is not clean
3. **(C)** "assimilationist"
4. **(D)** the untruths about Tarzan
5. **(C)** 20
6. **(A)** Alaiyo
7. **(A)** Walter
8. **(D)** a rat
9. **(C)** her identity
10. **(D)** to save Africans from heathanism
11. **(B)** Travis chasing a rat when playing with his friends
12. **(D)** Beneatha's medical school tuition and a house
13. **(A)** 2
14. **(A)** kitchen cleanser
15. **(A)** It demonstrates Walter's lack of knowledge
16. **(D)** Her hair is natural
17. **(B)** wanting to discard one's African past in order to gain acceptance amongst the white majority
18. **(B)** dancing
19. **(C)** surgery
21. **(C)** glasses
22. **(D)** He gets drunk
23. **(B)** She has placed a down payment on a new house
24. **(A)** The house is in a white neighborhood
25. **(C)** African–American

Quiz 3

1. **What is the central civil rights issue in the play?**
   A. school segregation
   B. employment discriminiation
   C. housing discrimination
   D. integration

2. **What aspect of the plot can be viewed as a deus ex machina?**
   A. Ruth's pregnancy
   B. the liquor store
   C. Mama's plant
   D. the insurance check

3. **The most likely explanation for why Travis may be described as 'spoiled' is because:**
   A. His father spends his entire paycheck on toys so that the young boy will not feel as if he is poor.
   B. Ruth is too focused on her pregnancy to discipline him properly.
   C. His grandmother never makes him do any chores.
   D. He has no strong authority figure and is able to play the adults off of one another.

4. **What is the first sound heard in the play?**
   A. the neighbors fighting for the bathroom
   B. an alarm clock
   C. a rooster
   D. Ruth yelling

5. **Who is the "head of the houshold" at the beginning of the play?**
   A. Walter
   B. Beneatha
   C. Mama
   D. Ruth

6. **Walter's goal of achieving wealth by opening a liquor store is best described as:**
   A. selfish
   B. classist
   C. communist
   D. entrepreneurial

7. **Walter fears:**

A. that his wife will leave him
B. that his son will go to college
C. that his mother will not allow him to invest the insurance money in the liquor store
D. that his mother is getting sick

8. **What does Ruth prepare for Walter for breakfast?**

A. cereal
B. oatmeal
C. scrambled eggs
D. poached eggs

9. **What does Walter not want for breakfast?**

A. oatmeal
B. scrambled eggs
C. poached eggs
D. grits

10. **In the first scene, why does Walter yell at Ruth?**

A. She makes him scrambled eggs
B. She is not listening to his dreams about the liquor store
C. She is pregnant and wants an abortion
D. She wants a divorce

11. **The Murchisons are what Asagai would call:**

A. assimiliationists
B. wealthy
C. privileged
D. upper–class

12. **When Mama asks, "Did he threaten us?" she is talking about:**

A. Walter
B. Lindner
C. Bobo
D. Willy

13. **Who says "Your're all wacked up with bitterness man?"**
    A. George Murchison
    B. Bobo
    C. Willy
    D. Asagai

14. **The title of the play was inspired by a poem by:**
    A. Sidney Poitier
    B. WEB Dubois
    C. Langston Hughes
    D. Lorraine Hansberry

15. **Lorraine Hansberry said that the character of Walter was inspired by:**
    A. The Death of a Salesman
    B. The Invisible Man
    C. Native Son
    D. Big White Fog

16. **At the end of the play:**
    A. the Youngers move into a bigger house in a black neighborhood
    B. the Youngers move to New York
    C. the Youngers leave to move into their house
    D. the Youngers remain in their apartment

17. **When Mama says, "He finally come into his manhood today, didn't he? Kind of like a rainbow after the rain," who is she talking about?**
    A. Travis
    B. Walter Jr.
    C. Walter Sr.
    D. Asagai

18. **Where does Asagai offer to take Beneatha?**
    A. his apartment
    B. Nigeria
    C. her family's new house
    D. Libya

19. **Who says, "I come from five generations of people who was slaves and sharecroppers but ain't nobody in my family never let nobody pay 'em no money that was a way of telling us we wasn't fit to walk the earth"?**
    A. Walter
    B. Beneatha
    C. Mama
    D. Ruth

20. **Whom does Walter work for?**
    A. Mr. Arnold
    B. Mr. Charles
    C. Mr. Lindner
    D. Mr. Murchison

21. **For how many days does Walter miss work?**
    A. 1
    B. 3
    C. 5
    D. 7

22. **What activity does Walter NOT do on the days that he misses work?**
    A. drive to Wisconsin and look at farms
    B. people–watch at 39th and South Parkway
    C. go to the Green Hat
    D. talk to Ruth about the pregnancy

23. **When cleaning up on Saturday morning, Beneatha is spraying for:**
    A. mice
    B. ants
    C. cockroaches
    D. none of the above

24. **How much is the down payment on the house?**
    A. $4,000
    B. $6,000
    C. $3,500
    D. $6,500

25. **By the end of the play, who is the "head of the family"?**
   A. Walter
   B. Travis
   C. Mama
   D. Ruth

Quiz 3 Answer Key

1. **(C)** housing discrimination
2. **(D)** the insurance check
3. **(D)** He has no strong authority figure and is able to play the adults off of one another.
4. **(B)** an alarm clock
5. **(C)** Mama
6. **(D)** entrepreneurial
7. **(C)** that his mother will not allow him to invest the insurance money in the liquor store
8. **(C)** scrambled eggs
9. **(B)** scrambled eggs
10. **(B)** She is not listening to his dreams about the liquor store
11. **(A)** assimiliationists
12. **(B)** Lindner
13. **(A)** George Murchison
14. **(C)** Langston Hughes
15. **(A)** The Death of a Salesman
16. **(C)** the Youngers leave to move into their house
17. **(B)** Walter Jr.
18. **(B)** Nigeria
19. **(C)** Mama
20. **(A)** Mr. Arnold
21. **(B)** 3
22. **(D)** talk to Ruth about the pregnancy
23. **(C)** cockroaches
24. **(C)** $3,500
25. **(A)** Walter

Quiz 4

1. **Who says, "Oh–so now it's life. Money is life. Once upon a time freedom used to be life"? And who is being spoken to?**
   A. Walter; Travis
   B. Lena; Walter
   C. Ruth; Walter
   D. Walter; Lena

2. **Who says, "You don't understand. It's all a matter of ideas, and God is just one idea I don't accept"?**
   A. Beneatha
   B. Mama
   C. Lena
   D. Ruth

3. **The name of the poem from which the play's title is taken:**
   A. "Harlem"
   B. "Justice"
   C. "Ennui"
   D. "Freedom's Law"

4. **Which of the following lines is NOT part of "Harlem"?**
   A. "Maybe it just sags/ Like a heavy load."
   B. "Does it dry up/ Like a raisin in the sun?"
   C. "What happens to a dream deferred?"
   D. "I have a dream"

5. **Identify the speaker and the subject matter of the following: "They don't do it like that any more. He talked Brotherhood."**
   A. Walter; the New Neighbors Oreientation Committee
   B. Beneatha; Asagai's marriage proposal
   C. Mama; the man who sold her the house
   D. Beneatha; Mr. Lindner's visit.

6. **Identify the following speaker: "We don't want your money."**
   A. Walter
   B. Travis
   C. Beneatha
   D. Ruth

7. **Why does Beneatha say, "I said that individual in that room is no brother of mine"?**
   A. Walter encorages Ruth to get an abortion
   B. Walter loses his job
   C. Walter loses the insurance money in a liquor store investment
   D. Walter wants Beneatha to become a nurse

8. **Who is Mama talking about when she says, "Have you cried for that boy today?"**
   A. George
   B. Walter
   C. Travis
   D. Willy

9. **What does Travis give Mama?**
   A. a gardening hat
   B. gardening tools
   C. a new plant
   D. none of the above

10. **What word does Beneatha repeat while dancing to African music?**
    A. OCOMOGOSIAY
    B. ALUNDI
    C. ALUNYA
    D. ANG GU SOOOOOOOO

11. **What time is the play George takes Beneatha to?**
    A. 8:00
    B. 8:10
    C. 8:30
    D. 8:40

12. **How much money does Walter put away for Beneatha's medical school?**
    A. $3,000
    B. $1,500
    C. $10,000
    D. none

13. **How much money does Mama ask Walter to put away for Beneatha's medical school education?**
   A. $3,000
   B. $5,000
   C. $6,500
   D. $10,000

14. **What do Ruth, Walter, and Beneatha get Lena for the new house?**
   A. new curtains
   B. a gardening hat
   C. gardening tools
   D. a new plant

15. **When Beneatha asks if her mother is going to take the old plant to the new house, she says:**
   A. "It expresses ME!"
   B. "Of course!"
   C. "Absolutely!"
   D. "Nah, maybe not."

16. **Why does Walter give Travis a dollar instead of fifty cents?**
   A. neither of the above
   B. Walter had borrowed some the money from him earlier in the week
   C. both of the above
   D. He does not want his son to worry about money

17. **What song does Mama ask Ruth to sing at the end of the first scene?**
   A. "I Got Wings"
   B. "Eye on the Sparrow"
   C. "No Ways Tired"
   D. "Amazing Grace"

18. **On what day does the insurance check come?**
   A. Friday
   B. Monday
   C. Saturday
   D. Thursday

19. **For how long have Ruth and Walter been married?**
    A. 8 years
    B. 10 years
    C. 11 years
    D. 15 years

20. **Who is Walter talking to when he says, "Here I am a giant – surrounded by ants! Ants who can't understand what it is the giant is talking about"?**
    A. George
    B. Beneatha
    C. Mr. Lindner
    D. Asagai

21. **What does Ruth offer her husband to help him get over his drunkenness?**
    A. neither of the above
    B. coffee
    C. hot milk
    D. both of the above

22. **How many bedrooms does the new house have?**
    A. 1
    B. 2
    C. 3
    D. 4

23. **Where is the new house?**
    A. Clybourne Park
    B. downtown
    C. the South Side of Chicago
    D. the location is never specified

24. **Where does Walter take his wife?**
    A. to the movies
    B. to the zoo
    C. to the park
    D. to the doctor

25. **Who tells Walter about the failed investment?**

A. Mr Atkins
B. Ms Johnson
C. Bobo
D. Willy

Quiz 4 Answer Key

1. **(B)** Lena; Walter
2. **(A)** Beneatha
3. **(A)** "Harlem"
4. **(D)** "I have a dream"
5. **(D)** Beneatha; Mr. Lindner's visit.
6. **(A)** Walter
7. **(C)** Walter loses the insurance money in a liquor store investment
8. **(B)** Walter
9. **(A)** a gardening hat
10. **(A)** OCOMOGOSIAY
11. **(C)** 8:30
12. **(D)** none
13. **(A)** $3,000
14. **(C)** gardening tools
15. **(A)** "It expresses ME!"
16. **(D)** He does not want his son to worry about money
17. **(C)** "No Ways Tired"
18. **(C)** Saturday
19. **(C)** 11 years
20. **(A)** George
21. **(D)** both of the above
22. **(C)** 3
23. **(A)** Clybourne Park
24. **(A)** to the movies
25. **(C)** Bobo

Made in the USA
Middletown, DE
14 December 2023